Lindisfarne Priory
and Holy Island

Eric Cambridge
UNIVERSITY OF DURHAM

Aerial view of the village, priory, harbour and castle beyond

NORTHUMBRIA AIRFOTOS

LINDISFARNE, later known as Holy Island, was the site of one of the most important early centres of Christianity in Anglo-Saxon England. Founded in 635 by St Aidan, first bishop of the northern Northumbrians, the monastery rapidly achieved international fame as a centre of learning and culture. After 698, when St Cuthbert's incorrupt body was enshrined in its church, Lindisfarne also became the pre-eminent cult centre of the north. The monastery fell prey to Viking raiders from the end of the eighth century, forcing the monks to seek safety on the mainland, taking Cuthbert's body with them.

Monks from Durham re-established a religious community here in the twelfth century; the priory, whose extensive ruins can still be seen, was built by them. A small community of monks lived here until the dissolution in 1537. Holy Island is still a place of pilgrimage today.

This Souvenir Guide opens with a tour of the medieval priory ruins. The tour is followed by an account of the Anglo-Saxon monastery and of the later priory, and a description of the monks' daily life in the later Middle Ages. These are followed by a brief portrayal of the monument's later history and the nearby royal defences.

1

Tour of the Priory

Drawing of carving of the Virgin and Child from the foot of St Cuthbert's coffin. The presence of the relics of St Cuthbert and other saints made Lindisfarne one of the great centres of pilgrimage in Anglo-Saxon England

DURHAM CATHEDRAL.

Priory Church

From the **museum**, turn right and walk along until you are facing the west front of the ruined priory church, with the east end of the parish church behind you. Though outside the remains of the twelfth-century and later monastery, you are probably standing near the centre of the site of its Anglo-Saxon predecessor. The location of the buildings of that early period is uncertain; our only clue is provided by the siting of these two later churches.

The ruined twelfth-century church in front of you was built on the site of a small seventh-century church housing St Cuthbert's shrine. Behind you is the more recent parish church of St Mary. It is largely of thirteenth-century date, but contains fragments of older, perhaps eleventh-century masonry, and may overlie another church of the Anglo-Saxon monastery.

Note how the two surviving churches are roughly in line with each other on an east-west axis, an arrangement typical of Anglo-Saxon monastic sites. The domestic buildings of the early monastery would probably have clustered around the sites of the two earlier churches.

Among the graves in this area is the large plain base of a free-standing **cross**. It may be of Anglo-Saxon date and in its original position. Perhaps it served as a focus of devotion for the early monks.

The **west front** of the ruined priory church must have been completed by around 1150. The richly decorated **west doorway** is contained in a slightly projecting porch. Above it is an opening which would originally have been concealed behind a steeply pitched gable, probably containing a tiny chamber over the doorway. There is an original window higher up, but the gable above that was rebuilt in the mid fourteenth century. Note the two cross-shaped arrow loops in this masonry, a reminder of the troubled times which followed the outbreak of the Scots wars in 1296. The **turret** on the left has

West front of the priory church, as it may have looked when first completed around 1150.

2   *A reconstruction by Terry Ball*

ENGLISH HERITAGE

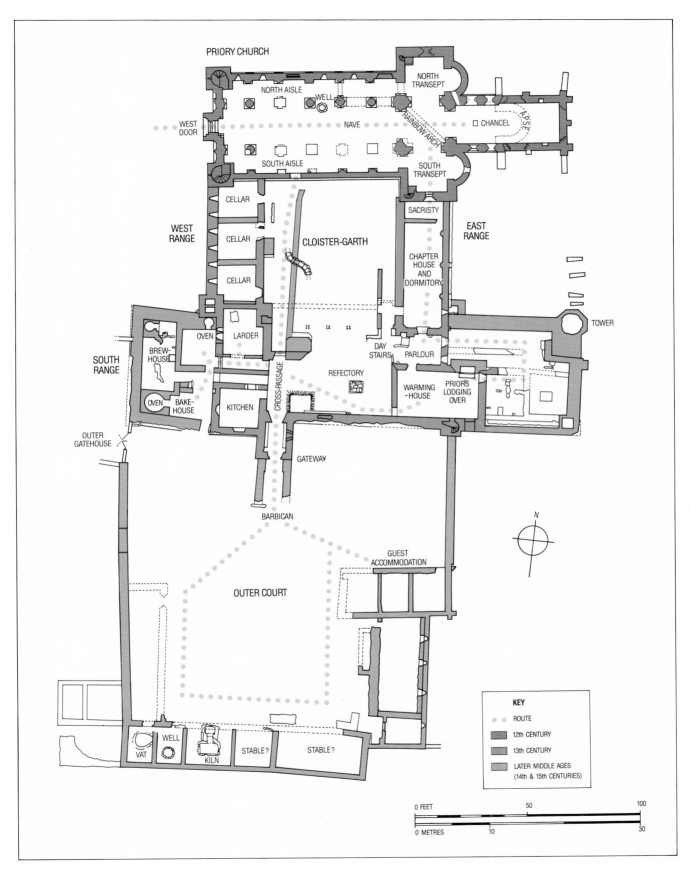

PRIORY CHURCH

NORTH TRANSEPT

NORTH AISLE

WELL

NAVE

RAINBOW ARCH

CHANCEL

APSE

WEST DOOR

SOUTH AISLE

SOUTH TRANSEPT

SACRISTY

CELLAR

WEST RANGE

CELLAR

CLOISTER-GARTH

CELLAR

EAST RANGE

CHAPTER HOUSE AND DORMITORY

TOWER

OVEN

LARDER

BREW-HOUSE

SOUTH RANGE

DAY STAIRS

PARLOUR

REFECTORY

OVEN

BAKE-HOUSE

KITCHEN

CROSS-PASSAGE

WARMING-HOUSE

PRIOR'S LODGING OVER

OUTER GATEHOUSE

GATEWAY

BARBICAN

GUEST ACCOMMODATION

N

OUTER COURT

VAT

WELL

KILN

STABLE?

STABLE?

KEY

ROUTE

12th CENTURY

13th CENTURY

LATER MIDDLE AGES (14th & 15th CENTURIES)

0 FEET   50   100

0 METRES   10   30

ABOVE *The priory church from the north-west. This view should be compared with the reconstruction on page 2*

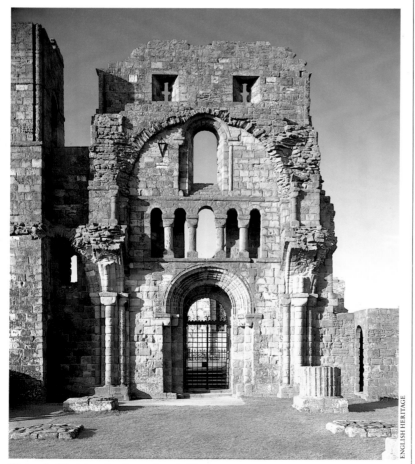

West wall of the priory church, seen from inside

been almost completely destroyed, but the one on the right survives nearly to full height. Each contained a spiral staircase leading to the upper parts of the church, and would have been capped by a pyramid shaped roof in the twelfth century, later replaced by flat roofs concealed behind battlements.

Enter the **nave** of the church via the west door, and note that the doorway was decorated with shafts inside as well as out — a very uncommon feature. Glance back at the inside of the west wall, noting the arcade of five small arches above the door, behind which is a wall-passage giving access to the chamber over the porch. Above are traces of the original vault. The entire church was vaulted in stone, an unusual and prestigious feature in an English medieval church. Above the vaults, the square openings behind the cross-shaped arrow loops can be seen. They were reached from a chamber formed above the vault in the fourteenth century.

The pillars of the nave are of two contrasting designs, one with groups of shafts, the other cylindrical with geometrical patterns incised on them. The upper parts of the nave walls have all been destroyed, but their form can be reconstructed from drawings made in the eighteenth and early nineteenth centuries. There was a gallery above the aisles, opening to the nave through paired arches, each pair surmounted by a tiny window tucked into the curve of the vault. The north aisle retains extensive traces of its vaulting. There was a single plain round-headed window in each bay, except where the north door (later blocked up) left room for only the tiniest of slits; a larger window was inserted in the easternmost bay around 1300.

There were probably two screens dividing off the western parts of the church from the eastern parts, where the monks held their services. Beam-holes in the pillars at the east end of the nave show where these were. The one to the west would have had an altar in the middle flanked by side doors. Above there would probably have been a beam carrying a crucifixion group. Foundations interpreted as bases for side altars have been discovered in front of the pillars at the east end of the nave.

Moving east from the nave, stand under the **crossing**, at the centre of the church. This was covered by a vault one of whose ribs miraculously survived the collapse of the tall twelfth-century central tower above at the end of the eighteenth century. It is popularly known as the **'rainbow arch'**. There were small arcaded passages running around each side of the tower similar to the one in the west wall of the nave. Only the arches leading into them can now be seen. The upper stage of the tower housed the monastery's bells, three in number at the end of

the Middle Ages. The stalls, or wooden seats for the monks, were probably underneath the tower. To north and south open the **transepts**, each covered by a vault like the one over the crossing, and each with a semi-circular apse opening out of its east wall. These would each have housed a side altar. Spiral stairs in the corner of each transept gave access to the upper parts of the church.

Move east to the **chancel**, and note the foundations of the main apse, the original east end of the church. It was demolished and the chancel doubled in size by the construction of an eastern extension later in the twelfth century. This is square ended, apses having gone out of fashion by this date. There are recesses opposite each other in the north and south walls near the east end. The square-headed recess in the north wall near the east end was probably a cupboard for the sacred vessels used during mass, and the trefoil-headed one opposite it in the south wall is a piscina, a drain used to dispose of the water in which the sacred vessels had been washed after mass was over. These features indicate that the

high altar was placed right at the east end of the new extension. The three large windows at this end were inserted later in the Middle Ages. None of the stone tracery which would have filled them survives, and the head of the east window is a modern replacement.

The spot where St Cuthbert had been buried and where his shrine had once rested would have been marked by a stone monument, probably in the form of a tomb-chest surmounted by a recumbent image of the saint in his bishop's robes, to judge from descriptions of similar cenotaphs elsewhere. We do not know where in the church this was. Perhaps it lay in the chancel, within the foundations of the original twelfth-century church. If so, this may explain the narrow passage leading from the chancel to the north transept apse, an unusual feature which might have been used as a means of access to Cuthbert's tomb by pilgrims.

Returning westwards to the crossing, turn left and leave the church by the door in the south wall of the south transept.

The priory church with, on the left, a decorated pillar of the nave and, centre, the 'rainbow arch' and crossing. Compare reconstruction on page 17

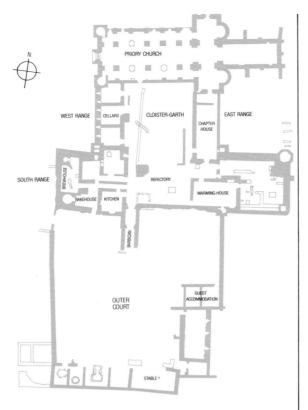

PRIORY CHURCH

WEST RANGE CELLARS CLOISTER-GARTH EAST RANGE

CHAPTER HOUSE

SOUTH RANGE

BREWHOUSE

REFECTORY

BAKEHOUSE KITCHEN

WARMING-HOUSE

BARBICAN

OUTER COURT

GUEST ACCOMMODATION

STABLE ?

Chimney-block inserted as part of the fourteenth-century reconstruction of the prior's apartments

Monastic Buildings

East Range

The earliest surviving buildings in which the monks lived were arranged, following the standard layout, enclosing three sides of an open square **cloister-garth**, the fourth being formed by the church itself. Lean-to corridors ran round the perimeter of the garth, connecting the three ranges of monastic buildings to each other and to the church. At Lindisfarne, these ranges seem to have been built from west to east, so the east range, in which you are standing, is the latest of them, of thirteenth-century date. The small room nearest the church served as the **sacristy**, where the chests containing vestments (the special robes the monks wore for services), and the community's small collection of relics of the saints were kept. The rest of the ground floor would have been used as the **chapter house**, where the monks met to discuss their business and commemorate their dead. Traces of the pillars and vaults supporting an upper floor can be seen. This would have housed the monks' **dormitory**. The door at the south end led to the **parlour**, where conversation was permitted.

Turn left and go through the doorway in the east wall of the parlour. From here the high defensive walls, erected in the troubled times of the early fourteenth century, rise up on all sides. The gap on the left leads to the remains of a much ruined **corner tower**; there was a smaller turret in the other outer corner. The foundations immediately within these walls are difficult to interpret. They are probably remains of the thirteenth-century **infirmary**, where sick or elderly monks were cared for.

Re-enter the buildings by the door into the **warming-house**, originally the only room where heating was allowed. The large chimney-block on the right, with fireplaces on the ground and first floors, was inserted in the fourteenth century, when this part of the buildings was extensively reconstructed. This room was probably used by the monks, while there were separate apartments for the **prior's lodging** above. The stairs to his principal room can be seen on the left. The prior also had a study and a chapel. These would have been smaller rooms, probably located north of his main room, above the parlour. From the mid fourteenth century these buildings, rather than the ranges round the cloister, became the focus of the life of the community, by then much reduced in size.

South Range

Go westwards into the slight remains of the south range of the buildings round the cloister. At first this range lay closer to the church, but was widened and rebuilt in its present position in the thirteenth century. The **refectory** or dining-hall of the monks would originally have been here; it was later taken over by the prior as his hall. Its square open hearth can be seen towards the middle of the floor area.

On the ground floor at the west end of the south range was a **cross-passage** with three thirteenth-century doorways in its west wall. These are the entrances to the services wing. Take the right-hand door and turn right into the **larder**. This has a pit in the floor; once lead-lined, it was perhaps for keeping foodstuffs cool. Beyond are rooms added in the mid fourteenth century. The one on the right contains a small brick-lined circular **oven**. The next is a **brewhouse**, with a sink in the floor and, in the corner, the remains of a kiln which would have heated a large brass vessel above. The third room is a **bakehouse**, with a large circular brick-lined oven. Near by in its south wall is a doorway to the outer court through which provisions and fuel would have been brought from the storehouses beyond. Return up the central passage and turn right into the **kitchen**, with the remains of two fireplaces. The second doorway from the kitchen brings you back to the cross-passage.

As well as being the way through which food and drink was brought from the services wing to the hall, the **cross-passage** connected the inner

parts of the monastery, which were the preserve of the monks, with the more public outer court to the south. There is a thirteenth-century **porch** at this end of the passage, where a porter would have kept out unauthorized visitors. It became a fortified **gateway** in the fourteenth century with the addition of a defensive **barbican** and, probably, an upper chamber. Pass through this gateway to the outer court.

Outer Court

At Lindisfarne, the perimeter of a monastic outer court and its buildings is unusually well-preserved. Go first to the south-east corner, where the **guest accommodation** comprised an upper-floor hall in the centre, with service rooms to the left and a small chamber opening off the opposite end. The next building, in the south range, may have been a **stable**, with hay loft above. Further west is a room containing a **kiln**, probably for drying corn, followed by a room housing a **well** and, in the south-west corner, another with the remains of a **vat**, perhaps connected with tanning or brewing.

It is easy to forget that the priory needed to be almost entirely self-sufficient so that, besides the various functions listed above, the outer court would have contained buildings such as storage barns for cereals, haystacks, woodpiles, a smithy, and accommodation for domestic animals, particularly cows, pigs, and fowl. Presumably there were more buildings than are now visible. Some, perhaps, were free-standing in the court, while there are traces of others along the west perimeter wall. All in all, this area would have been a busy, muddy farmyard in the Middle Ages, very different from the neat expanse of lawn seen today.

The west wall of the court has a **walkway** along the top with battlements, presumably fourteenth-century in date, like the other priory defences. In the north-west corner is the site of the **outer gatehouse**, the main entrance to the monastery in the Middle Ages.

West Range

Return through the inner gatehouse and cross-passage to the cloister. On the left is the west range, the first part of the existing monastic buildings to be constructed, most likely in the late twelfth century. Its **ground floor** was divided into three vaulted rooms in the four-teenth century. These would have been used as cellars for storing various provisions, notably wine, and for keeping the table linen and utensils used in the hall. The **first floor** may originally have been the prior's lodging. Later it probably housed more important guests.

From here return to the nave of the church and leave by the west door.

A general view of the priory from the south. Note the strong defensive walls of the outer court in the foreground and the thirteenth-century parish church on the left

History of Lindisfarne

Origins

The monastery on Lindisfarne was founded in 635 by Aidan, an Irish monk summoned by King Oswald of Northumbria to be the first missionary bishop of Bernicia, as the northern part of his kingdom was then known. Aidan came from the island monastery of Iona, in what is now south-west Scotland. Perhaps this is why he chose an island site for his community. Another reason would have been closeness to the royal fortress at Bamburgh, six miles south on the Northumberland coast, early missionaries being directly dependent on the support and protection of kings.

Iona had been founded by the great Irish saint Columba, and Aidan perpetuated the ascetic traditions of Irish monasticism at Lindisfarne. 'Frugal and austere' was how the historian Bede later described his regime.

If the evidence of later Irish monasteries is anything to go by, Aidan's buildings were probably small and simple, consisting of individual cells housing one or two monks — perhaps a master and a novice — grouped irregularly round the church. It is likely that this area would have been divided off in some way from other more public buildings, such as the guest house; the whole complex would probably have been enclosed, perhaps by a low bank and ditch. Aidan's successor as bishop, Finan, built a church in the Irish tradition, of hewn oak covered with reed thatch, which became the principal church

St Cuthbert's Island, the site of a seventh-century hermitage. Still visible are the ruins of a later medieval chapel

of the community and was dedicated to St Peter. The thatch was later replaced by lead sheets.

Like other early monasteries, the buildings were not all grouped close together; outlying hermitages were also established from the earliest days, on St Cuthbert's Island, a quarter of a mile south-west of the present priory site, and on the uninhabited island of Inner Farne, seven miles to the south.

The patronage of kings and the presence of a bishop's seat would themselves have ensured Lindisfarne's fame. But its future was about to be transformed by the life and death of its greatest saint, Cuthbert.

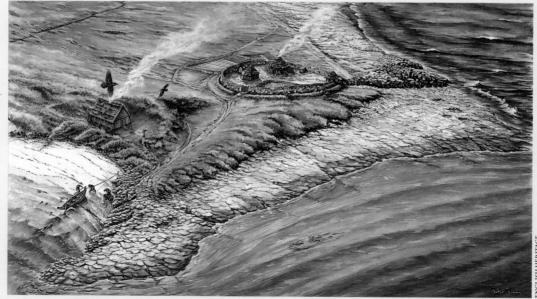

Cuthbert's hermitage on Inner Farne, as it may have appeared in the late seventh century. A reconstruction by Peter Dunn

Aerial view of Holy Island from the south. The offshore island site gave isolation to the seventh-century monastery, yet easy access to the mainland and to the nearby royal fortress of Bamburgh

Cuthbert

A native Anglo-Saxon, Cuthbert trained in the monastery of Melrose (now in southern Scotland) under its abbot, Eata, who had been trained by Aidan himself, and its prior, Boisil. When Eata became abbot (and later bishop) of Lindisfarne, Cuthbert moved there with him as prior. His reputation for personal holiness, already considerable, was much increased as a result of his withdrawal (like Aidan before him) to become a hermit on the Inner Farne, which was not just a tranquil refuge from worldly distractions, but was thought of as a wild and dangerous place, the preserve of evil spirits. As well as being physically tough, the life of a hermit was thus seen also as a spiritual battle with the devil himself, a battle in which only a few monks were capable of engaging.

Much against his will, Cuthbert eventually agreed to succeed Eata as bishop in 685, exchanging his solitary life for one which entailed a heavy burden of pastoral responsibilities and involved constant travelling about his large diocese. Within two years, realising that his end was near, he retired

Seventh-century gold cross set with garnets. The cross was probably owned and worn by Cuthbert

again to Farne to die.

Cuthbert's body was brought back to Lindisfarne and buried on the right of the altar in St Peter's church in March 687. Eleven years later, in 698, the monks dug up the remains, expecting to recover bones and dust to be enshrined in a small casket. Instead, much to their surprise, they discovered Cuthbert's body completely undecayed. That fact was to alter the entire course of the history of the community.

The body was placed in a hastily prepared wooden reliquary-coffin, and set on the floor of the church above where it had been buried. Astonishingly, substantial parts of that coffin still exist today, together with other precious objects associated with the saint; they are preserved at Durham Cathedral, his final resting-place. The survival of a group of objects associated with an early and well-documented saint's cult is unique in Europe.

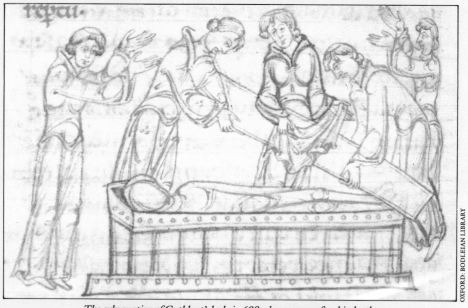

The exhumation of Cuthbert's body in 698, eleven years after his death, as depicted in a twelfth-century manuscript. Miraculously, the body was found to be undecayed

Drawings of carvings on St Cuthbert's coffin. TOP *Archangels.* BOTTOM *Christ and the four Evangelist symbols on the lid*

Late twelfth-century wall-painting at Durham Cathedral of a bishop, probably St Cuthbert

The Lindisfarne Gospels

Besides the relics themselves, one other famous object survives from the early monastery. The Lindisfarne Gospels, produced either for the enshrinement of 698 or in response to it, show the extraordinary technical skill which the monastery had already attained in the making of books. The scribe was a monk named Eadfrith, who became bishop of Lindisfarne in *c*698. Such precious objects were often made by the monks themselves in this period, the exercise of artistic skill then being regarded as a form of devotion. The large number of calf-hides which were needed to produce the parchment on which it is written — perhaps one for every two of its 258 pages — indicates the substantial resources then at the community's disposal.

FLORENCE: BIBLIOTECA MEDICEA-LAURENZIANA

In the Codex Amiatinus, a bible produced at Wearmouth-Jarrow about 700, the scribe Ezra is shown writing, surrounded by the tools of his craft

Eighth Century

The miracles that occurred at Cuthbert's shrine soon established Lindisfarne as the major pilgrimage centre of Northumbria, and a sought-after burial place. As a result, the monastery rapidly grew in power and wealth, attracting grants of land from kings and nobles as well as gifts of money and precious objects. King Ceolwulf, who retired to become a monk there in 737, was later remembered as a particularly generous benefactor.

The prestige of Cuthbert's relics also had less desirable side effects, however, as criminals and

political refugees fled to their protection. Around 756 for example, Offa, an unsuccessful pretender to the kingship, was dragged half-dead from the church by his pursuers, and bishop Cynewulf imprisoned at Bamburgh. The community thus became involved willy-nilly in Northumbrian politics. Its religious life must also have been disrupted by constantly having to entertain large numbers of visitors, particularly as the royal and aristocratic ones presumably expected hospitality in the style to which they were accustomed. Worse still, increased wealth may have led to a decline in the standards of monastic observance. There are already dark hints of this from Bede, writing in the 730s. And a later Northumbrian scholar, Alcuin, was perhaps not just observing theological convention when he interpreted the Viking raid on Lindisfarne in 793 as God's judgement on the luxurious life style of the monks.

All this means that, by the end of the eighth century, the monastery must have been very different in appearance from the few humble buildings of Aidan's time. It was presumably much bigger for one thing; and some of its buildings may well have been reconstructed more grandly in stone. Even so, they would have seemed small and simple compared with the buildings to be seen on the site today, for, unlike their Norman successors, Anglo-Saxon churchmen were generally more interested in owning richly ornamented objects — books, church plate, embroideries — than in constructing monumental buildings. Marvellous as the surviving treasures from Lindisfarne are, they must represent only a tiny fraction of the riches that the monastery must have accumulated by the end of the eighth century. Those riches were to prove its undoing.

MARSHALL-TIVEY (IMAGES COLOUR LIBRARY)

The present Bamburgh Castle, which was built on the historic site of the great stronghold of the Northumbrian kings

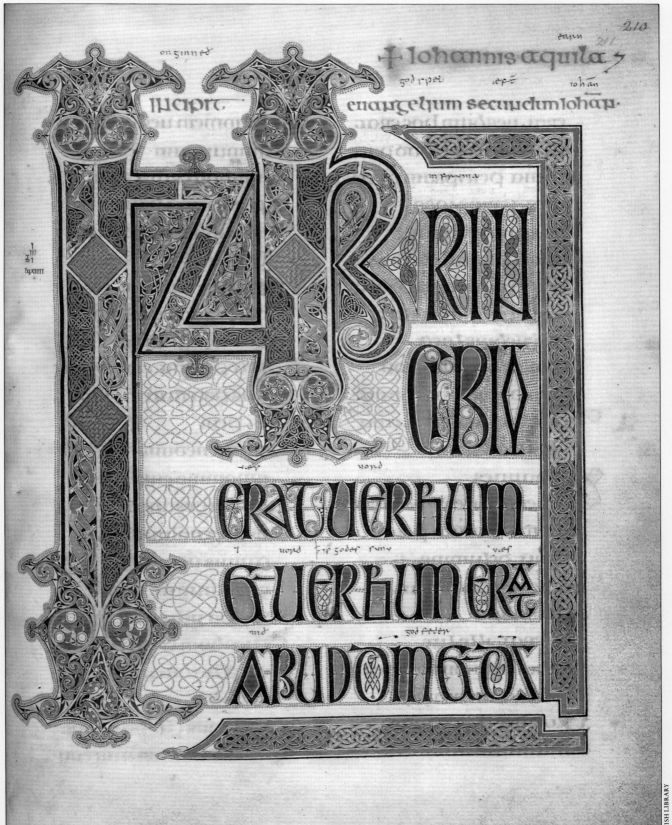

Vikings and After

In 793, the church of Lindisfarne was destroyed by 'the heathen'. News of the assault was greeted with horror as far away as the court of Charlemagne, then the greatest ruler in western Europe; the new era of Viking raids had begun. To pagan Vikings, isolated monasteries — in effect undefended treasure-houses — were easy pickings; and Lindisfarne's location made it particularly vulnerable. The monks seem to have survived that first assault, but within a generation, the community was forced to leave the island, taking with them the relics of Cuthbert and their other saints, and the body of King Ceolwulf. Even the timber church of St Peter — presumably by now regarded as a kind of relic in its own right — was dismantled and re-erected at their first refuge, Norham, on the Tweed. But even Norham had become too insecure by the later ninth century, and

St Cuthbert's relics being carried across the sands to Lindisfarne in 1069: a twelfth-century manuscript illustration

the community had to move yet again. At one point it seemed poised to take refuge in Ireland, but eventually settled at Chester-le-Street in 883, some sixty miles south of its original home. The final move to Durham, a few miles further down the road, took place in or shortly after 995.

Great though the fame of the early monastery had been, it represents from an archaeological point of view a comparatively brief interlude in the settlement history of the island. The monastery survived for just about two centuries, only half the span of its medieval successor.

The departure of the monks did not mean that religious life on the island ceased altogether. A church serving the local population presumably survived, probably on the site of the present parish church, which contains masonry perhaps of eleventh-century date. And the former monastery must have continued to act as an important focus for burial, which would account for the large number of carved stones apparently dating from this period which have been found on the priory site.

Cuthbert's body was to return only once more to the island, when the Anglo-Saxon clergy fled there from Durham after the Norman Conquest, in 1069-70, but its stay was short. It has rested in Durham Cathedral ever since.

The frontispiece of a book containing two versions of St Cuthbert's life (c 930) shows King Athelstan presenting that book to the saint at Chester-le-Street

The priory ruins and the village from across the harbour

A grave-marker of about 900, carved with scenes depicting the onset of Doomsday. On one side the Cross appears in the heavens; on the other, a procession of armed warriors (shown perhaps as Viking raiders)

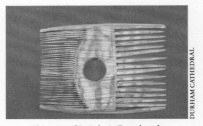

TOP *This copy of St John's Gospel, only 5¼ in (135 mm) tall, was made about 700 at Wearmouth-Jarrow and is still in its contemporary leather binding: found in Cuthbert's coffin in 1104 along with other relics, including the ivory comb below*

Eighth-century cross-shaft with interlaced animal decoration also found in the Lindisfarne Gospels

A grave-marker or 'name-stone' commemorating one Osgyth, one of the earliest surviving carvings at Lindisfarne (perhaps c700)

One of the many tenth-century cross-shafts at Lindisfarne. The symbolism of the figures is uncertain, but the central figure may represent Christ on the Day of Judgement

Refoundation

By the early twelfth century the cult of St Cuthbert at Durham, boosted by the translation of his relics into the magnificent new Norman Cathedral in 1104, was at its height. That cathedral was now staffed by a newly founded community of Benedictine monks, who rapidly became interested in the holy places anciently associated with their patron saint: his burial place on Holy Island and the site of the hermitage on Farne where he had died. These, especially Farne, were frequently visited by pilgrims from the north. A Durham presence on Holy Island was established by a monk called Edward in the early twelfth century, and other Durham monks, Bartholemew and Thomas, went to live as hermits on Farne shortly after 1150. For the next four centuries the history of these places was inseparable from that of the great cathedral-priory of Durham.

The priory church on Holy Island was constructed, probably in the second quarter of the twelfth century, to provide a fitting setting for the cenotaph marking the place where, according to tradition, Cuthbert's coffin had been placed in the Anglo-Saxon church. The monk Edward is described as having erected a church over that spot. This is often assumed to be the existing ruins, but could refer to an earlier structure.

Distinctive details of the architecture, such as the patterns incised on the cylindrical pillars of the nave, and provision of stone vaults throughout, demonstrate that the church was designed and built by masons sent up from Durham Cathedral. (Building was generally carried out by professional

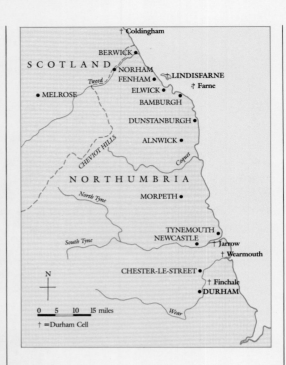

The nave of Durham Cathedral, built in c 1110-33

ROY REED (TRIANGLE TWO)

masons by this time, and would not have been done by the monks themselves). Indeed, the whole design looks like a miniature version of Durham, even down to dividing the walls of the nave into three stages, though these could scarcely be squeezed in beneath the vaults. Durham masons may have been employed simply because masons were hard to come by in the north at that time; yet the possibility that the appearance of the church which housed Cuthbert's shrine was being deliberately emulated in this outpost of his cult cannot be ignored.

The church at Lindisfarne was evidently completed some time before any of the extant monastic buildings were begun. This is the reverse of the usual order in which monasteries were constructed; normally, some permanent accommodation for the monks was built before starting work on the church. The special significance of Lindisfarne in St Cuthbert's cult probably explains why the church was given such a high priority here. What is more, the church looks as though it was originally meant to have been free-standing, whereas by this date monastic churches were directly connected to the domestic buildings. Presumably the monks were at first too few to make it worth building accommodation arranged in the standard pattern of three ranges surrounding a square cloister adjoining the church; probably they lived instead in simpler buildings more like an ordinary dwelling-house, and perhaps at first of timber. The eventual construction of buildings on the standard plan around 1200 suggests that the community had quickly increased in numbers; the eastward extension of the church may also reflect the needs of an expanding community.

The nave of the priory church as it may have appeared in the later Middle Ages. A reconstruction by Terry Ball. Compare photograph on page 16

Cells

Holy Island priory was only one of a large network of cells, or satellite monasteries directly controlled by the prior of the mother-house at Durham; they were a distinctive feature of the life of the Durham monks. All monks serving in the cells would have been trained at Durham, and were sent out, moved from one cell to another, or recalled to the mother-house, as the prior of Durham thought fit. Generally, monks were moved around often, every two or three years on average. This would curb any temptation to flout the Durham prior's authority; spells back in the mother-house would doubtless also strengthen a flagging sense of vocation. A few monks nevertheless stayed at a cell for long periods; perhaps they had family connections in the area, or simply preferred the quieter form of life. A likely example of the former is Gilbert of Elwick, who served as prior for an exceptionally long spell (1328-50). If his name is any indication, he came from Elwick, a small settlement opposite the island on the mainland.

Cells varied greatly in size, from Farne Island, which never had more than one or two monks, to Coldingham (north of Berwick), where the community numbered over thirty monks in the thirteenth century. Lindisfarne, to judge by the size of the monastic buildings, must have fallen between these two extremes, though it probably never attained the thirteen monks deemed necessary for leading a fully monastic life.

War and its Aftermath

Around 1300 the priory became caught up in a series of events which were to bring about dramatic and permanent changes in its fortunes. After Edward I's invasion of Scotland in 1296, the border, hitherto a peaceful and prosperous area, became an economically depressed and chronically insecure frontier zone. The income of the cell, all derived from nearby estates, shrank dramatically from its thirteenth-century levels, and never recovered. In 1327, one of the monks lamented that the tithes of Holy Island parish, which provided the greater part of their income, were worth only £21 that year; 'before the war', they had been worth as much as £127 a year. Declining income was reflected in shrinking numbers, so that only two or three monks could be supported by the early fifteenth century, compared with perhaps as many as ten before the troubles. But the wars had even more direct consequences: the monks were obliged to provide for their own defence.

Major changes to the priory buildings took place in the mid fourteenth century to adapt them to the changed circumstances. The church was fortified by constructing chambers provided with arrow-loops (still visible at the top of the west front) above the north aisle and the high vaults; and battlements were built on the tops of the walls. A strong wall and tower were built east of the prior's lodging, and an outer defence or barbican added to the gate-passage between the cloisters and the outer court. Lists of armour, weapons, and ammunition kept in store begin to appear in priory documents. The new fortifications evidently proved to be a liability at times, however. In 1385, the monks asked the king's permission to take them down, because they could not afford to provide a garrison to man them.

The regular plan of the monastic buildings based on the cloister was also abandoned in favour of domestic arrangements more convenient for the smaller community. The central focus now became the prior's lodging, whose chamber and great hall, together with some of its service buildings, were reconstructed at this time. But not all the alterations were prompted by necessity, new windows being inserted into the church and its statues repainted.

Fourteenth-century fortifications protecting the prior's lodging. Note the projecting corner-turret

Holy Island at low tide, showing the modern causeway. The pilgrims' path led across the sands to the right of the modern road

Daily Life in the later Middle Ages

Despite their reduced numbers, monks in the later Middle Ages would have continued to follow the tightly organised daily routine prescribed by their calling. They normally attended seven services together in the church every day, the times regulated by a mechanical clock; in addition, each said daily mass privately at a side altar. The conscientious regular worship of God is perhaps the hardest aspect of daily life for the present-day visitor to recapture, yet it remained the central concern of the monks throughout the priory's existence. Worship somehow also had to be combined with the practical administration of the priory's affairs. The prior had overall control of the little community. He would appoint one of the monks as cellarer, to look after the supplies of food and drink; another must have acted as sacrist, arranging the church services.

A cellarer tests his brew. From a thirteenth-century manuscript

Monastic routine was more severely disrupted when the monks' duties took them outside the walls of the monastery altogether. For example, there was the collection of their revenues and the management of their property, notably the manor at Fenham, opposite the priory on the mainland, where many of the monks' basic foodstuffs were produced. Durham priory's own revenues from the region were generally looked after by a monk from Holy Island too. There would also be occasional business trips to local towns such as Berwick (at least when not in Scottish hands), where a mason or carpenter might be hired to carry out building repairs. Besides, the prior had to travel to Durham every year to present his accounts at the annual chapter meeting there, and no doubt took the opportunity to do business at towns further afield, notably

Newcastle, the region's principal port. Here he might have bought imported goods, such as timber from the Baltic, iron, lead, spices and wine, and arranged to have them shipped back to Holy Island.

From time to time a messenger would arrive at the priory with a letter from Durham, perhaps announcing that one of the monks was to leave for a spell of service elsewhere. Pilgrims were probably few and far between by the later Middle Ages, but St Cuthbert's two feast days, on March 20 and September 4, would have perhaps continued to attract numbers of local people, who came to pray at the saint's burial place and venerate his staff, the principal relic kept at the priory. Occasionally, there would be the excitement of the arrival of an important visitor; at other times, panic at the sound of the alarm-bell, indicating that Scots raiders were close by. At such times the local villagers and their livestock were presumably allowed to take refuge in the outer court.

Acute though its own difficulties often were, Holy Island priory seems to have been more secure than Durham's other two cells in the area, Coldingham and Farne, taking in fellow-monks from those places when misfortune temporarily made them uninhabitable. Similarly, local parish priests took refuge there on occasion. From the late fifteenth century, the guest-rooms were apparently less frequently required, and were let out to paying guests, providing a small amount of extra income.

For all its insecurities, daily life in the late medieval monastery was not generally lacking in comforts. The monks still employed numerous domestic servants, who outnumbered them by at least two to one; in many ways, they lived like country gentlemen. Following the fourteenth-century alterations, they would have enjoyed more personal privacy than before, which may have helped to compensate for a waning of community spirit following the decrease in numbers. And payments to minstrels show that the great festivals of the Church's year were still occasions for convivial celebration.

It was hardly an atmosphere likely to generate saints; perhaps more surprisingly, it gave rise to few sinners. Discipline among the monks did, admittedly, need correction on occasion. The young monks in Gilbert of Elwick's time were ticked off by the prior of Durham for showing insolence rather than respect to their elderly superior. And a later prior of Durham wrote in 1465 complaining that the monks were wearing woollen rather than linen clothes (surely excusable on a windswept island!), playing sports, frequenting public houses, straying outside the monastery without permission, and telling risqué jokes; but serious lapses of discipline were very rare. Most of the criticisms suggest that some of the monks found life in this outpost of Durham's empire rather dull, which may help to explain why most did not stay for long.

The priory church and cloister-garth as they may have appeared in the later Middle Ages. The west range is on the left. Reconstruction by Terry Ball

A similar view today. The southern half of the nave has gone, exposing the pillars of the north arcade. The cloister-garth is in the foreground and the foundations of the west range on the left

Change and Decay: the Reformation and after

At the Reformation in 1537, the priory was closed by Henry VIII's commissioners. At first its buildings and estates continued under Durham ownership, and were leased to the last prior, Thomas Sparke. He, in turn, sub-let it to the Crown, which assumed control of the property.

The priory buildings seem to have become disused by the early seventeenth century, and the lead was stripped from the roofs in about 1613. The ruination of the buildings was gradual, much of the church surviving into the eighteenth century. Its progressive decay can be charted in a series of drawings and engravings. Most of the nave and the central tower collapsed between 1780 and 1820. Parts of the buildings were deliberately demolished by the islanders 'to serve as sand for their houses' according to one local historian. On the credit side, the site came into the hands of an enlightened owner, Mr Selby, who cleared the site of rubble and repaired the surviving ruins in the 1820s, thus preventing further decay. The large buttresses at the east end belong to his time. Much of the west front collapsed in the 1850s, and was carefully rebuilt by the Crown at considerable expense. Without such efforts, far less would be preserved today. The monastic buildings were excavated by Sir William Crossman, the lord of the manor, in 1887-89.

Royal Defences

Even before the end of the priory, the Crown was engaged in drawing Holy Island into its network of border defences. The harbour to the east of the priory made an ideal shelter for shipping, and a place where provisions could be unloaded, stored, and distributed. The priory buildings, including the church itself, were used as storehouses in the mid sixteenth century.

Three temporary earth and timber defences were erected in the area of the harbour in 1542-45, and a fourth on the site of the present castle in 1548-49; a grandiose scheme to refortify the entire priory site at this time came to nothing. After much complaining from the captain, Sir William Read, the castle was reconstructed in stone between 1565 and 1571 to protect the harbour, at a cost of over a thousand pounds. A small garrison was kept there until 1819, but rarely saw action when peace returned to the area following the union of the crowns of England and Scotland in 1603, except for brief periods during the Civil War and the Jacobite rebellion of 1715. The castle later served as a coastguard station. Its remains were converted into a holiday retreat for the proprietor of *Country Life* by the famous architect Sir Edwin Lutyens from 1902. It is now administered by the National Trust.

A second fort, called Osborne's fort, was built at Steel End, opposite the castle on the priory side of the harbour, in the 1670s. Today only the foundations of its central redoubt and traces of the perimeter walls are visible. It is rare for the remains of a fort of this type and date to survive unmodified by later reconstruction, which gives them an importance far greater than their present unprepossessing appearance might suggest.

ENGLISH HERITAGE

Lindisfarne castle from across the harbour. The sixteenth-century castle was restored and converted into a private house from 1902

Archaeology of the Island

Venerable though the Christian associations of Lindisfarne are, religious settlement must represent only a tiny part of the history of human activity on the island. Surprisingly little is known about this, but recent fieldwork and excavation, led by Deirdre O'Sullivan and Robert Young, are beginning to fill in some of the gaps. At Green Shiel, on the north coast, a site showing domestic occupation dating from the late ninth and tenth centuries AD has been excavated, and provides valuable confirmation that the Viking raids did not mean the end of all occupation of the island. At the other end of the time-scale, a survey nearby at Nessend quarry has revealed flint working over a long period from c8000 to 1500 BC. This is the earliest evidence of human activity yet identified on the island, dating in part from before rising sea-levels had even created the island as we know it today.

ABOVE *An illustration of c 1673, showing the harbour defences from the south. On the left are Osborne's Fort and the priory ruins. To the right is the castle*

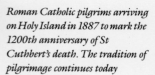

Roman Catholic pilgrims arriving on Holy Island in 1887 to mark the 1200th anniversary of St Cuthbert's death. The tradition of pilgrimage continues today

An early photograph of the priory church undergoing excavations and repairs in 1913

In this Victorian mural, King Egfrid is shown persuading Cuthbert to forsake his hermitage on Farne and become a bishop. Painted in 1856 by William Bell Scott at Wallington Hall, near Morpeth. Note the pair of Eiders and ducklings at Cuthbert's feet and the Arctic Terns circling overhead

Natural World

The monks of Lindisfarne must often have been aware of the island's remarkable natural environment. St Cuthbert's mysterious power over the natural world is a prominent theme in early accounts of his life. By the twelfth century the Eider duck had become particularly closely associated with him in tradition. It was presumably an Eider duck that the monks of Durham were sufficiently concerned to have accurately depicted on their great new screen behind the high altar of Durham Cathedral that, in 1380, they specially commissioned a Newcastle painter to produce a 'bird of St Cuthbert' as a model for their own craftsmen. Today several pairs of Eider still breed on Holy Island, though the largest colony is to be found on the Farnes, which is one of their most southerly breeding locations.

In the winter months the tidal sand and mud flats between the island and the mainland provides one of Britain's most important feeding grounds for visiting flocks of wildfowl and waders.

The vegetation of the island is transitional between species with characteristically northern and southern distributions; for example, Sea Purslane is not found north of here, and Grass of Parnassus only rarely farther south. The salt-marsh and dune environment supports some rare species. The range of orchids is noteworthy. The Northern Marsh Orchid and Marsh Helleborine are particularly beautiful. More commonly, Marram Grass is widespread on the sand dunes, Cord Grass dominates the salt marsh and Eel Grass is an important grass grazed by wildfowl in the intertidal areas. In the south of the island, the Sea Pink or Thrift provides a carpet of colour.